Celebrating Cultures

Mardi Gras

Jill Foran

New Hanover County Public Library
201 Chestnut Street
Wilmington, NC 28401

WEIGL PUBLISHERS INC.

Published by Weigl Publishers Inc.
123 South Broad Street, Box 227
Mankato, MN, 56002, USA
Web site: www.weigl.com

Library of Congress Cataloging-in-Publication Data

Foran, Jill.
  Mardi Gras / Jill Foran.
      p. cm. -- (Celebrating cultures)
Includes index.
Summary: Provides information on the pre-Lenten festival of Mardi Gras,
focusing on how it is celebrated in New Orleans.
  ISBN 1-59036-093-1 (lib. bdg. : alk. paper)
 1. Carnival--Louisiana--New Orleans--Juvenile literature. 2.
Carnival--United States--Juvenile literature. 3. New Orleans
(La.)--Social life and customs--Juvenile literature. [1. Mardi Gras. 2.
Festivals.] I. Title.
  GT4211.N4 F67 2003
  394.25--dc21

                            2002014570

Printed in the United States of America
1 2 3 4 5 6 7 8 9 0   06 05 04 03 02

Project Coordinator Janice Redlin **Design & Layout** Bryan Pezzi
Copy Editor Diana Marshall **Photo Researcher** Wendy Cosh

Contents

A Big Party

Mardi Gras is the biggest party of the year.

Mardi Gras is the biggest party of the year for millions of Americans. A season called Carnival begins on January 6. Carnival lasts until the day called Mardi Gras. Mardi Gras is the last day of fun for **Christians** before Ash Wednesday. Ash Wednesday marks the beginning of **Lent**. Lent occurs between February 3 and March 9.

Mardi Gras is a lively, colorful celebration.

Many festivities are held during Carnival. **Krewes** organize dozens of costume balls. Everyone is welcome to see the parades in the streets. Many bands play local music, including jazz, **Cajun**, blues, and gospel.

Carnival can last 4 to 8 weeks. The length of the season depends on the date of Mardi Gras each year.

January

Sun	Mon	Tues	Wed	Thur	Fri	Sat
		1	2	3	4	5
6 Carnival begins	7	8	9	10	11	12
13	14	15				
20	21	22				
27	28	29				

February

Sun	Mon	Tues	Wed	Thur	Fri	Sat
					1	2
3	4	5	6	7	8	9
10	11	12 Mardi Gras	13 Ash Wednesday	14	15	16
17	18	19	20	21	22	23
24	25	26	27	28		

e date of Mardi Gras
ries from year to year.

The Meaning of Mardi Gras

"Fat Tuesday" was a day of fun and feasting.

Mardi Gras means "Fat Tuesday" in the French language. Mardi Gras was a time of enjoyment and feasting in old Europe. It was celebrated before Lent began on Ash Wednesday. People fasted during Lent. This means that they gave up certain foods and **luxuries** to help them concentrate on their religion. People living in Paris, France, hundreds of years ago would parade a fattened bull through the city's streets on Mardi Gras. This show reminded everyone not to eat meat during Lent.

People eat pastries and miniature pizzas during Mardi Gras.

French **settlers** moved to North America. They continued to honor Mardi Gras traditions in their new country. French settlements in the southern United States have celebrated Mardi Gras every year since 1699. Mardi Gras was so much fun that other Americans celebrated the event.

The first American Mardi Gras was celebrated in Mobile, Alabama, in 1703.

Dancing is a popular activity during Mardi Gras.

Today's Mardi Gras parades often include large ceramic bulls.

A Club Celebration

Fancy parades became a part of Carnival celebrations.

In 1857, six men formed a special Carnival club in New Orleans, Louisiana. On Mardi Gras night, the men wore costumes and paraded two small **floats**. People carrying torches walked beside the floats. The crowds loved the show. Soon, fancy parades became a regular part of Carnival celebrations.

The Rex Mardi Gras parade has a very long tradition of attracting large crowds.

Today there are more than sixty krewes based in New Orleans. Some krewes have been created for dog and cat owners. Other krewes have only women for members. There are many other types of krewes as well. Some krewes are only 10 years old. Others have been together for more than 100 years.

Krewes were once very secretive. Many krewes would only admit certain people based on race or social status. The city of New Orleans made a rule that **discrimination** is not allowed.

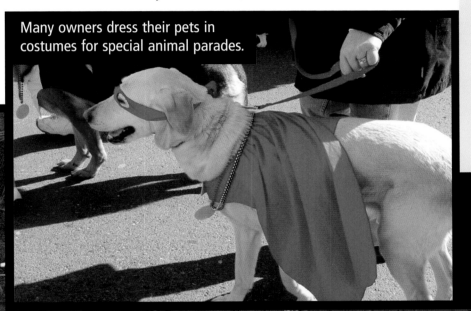

Many owners dress their pets in costumes for special animal parades.

Most Mardi Gras floats have specific subjects. This float is all about cats.

Mardi Gras in New Orleans

New Orleans hosts the largest Mardi Gras party in North America.

Every year, thousands of people travel to New Orleans for Mardi Gras. The city hosts the largest Mardi Gras celebration in North America. The residents of New Orleans decorate their city with colorful streamers when Carnival begins. The city stays decorated throughout the season.

Hundreds of people line the streets to watch

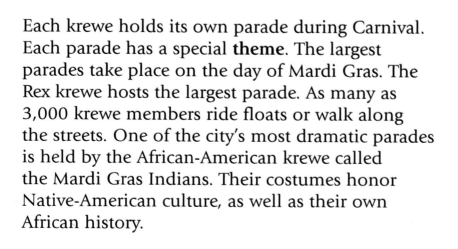

Each krewe holds its own parade during Carnival. Each parade has a special **theme**. The largest parades take place on the day of Mardi Gras. The Rex krewe hosts the largest parade. As many as 3,000 krewe members ride floats or walk along the streets. One of the city's most dramatic parades is held by the African-American krewe called the Mardi Gras Indians. Their costumes honor Native-American culture, as well as their own African history.

Most Mardi Gras balls follow a krewe's theme. Krewe members perform plays for their guests. The plays are taken from history, legends, and books.

Each member of the Mardi Gras Indian krewe creates their own unique costume.

Dressing up in fancy costumes and masks is part of the Mardi Gras tradition.

Americans Celebrate

New Orleans hosts the best-known Mardi Gras celebration. Many other cities hold Mardi Gras parties as well. This map reveals the many other important Mardi Gras traditions in the United States.

The largest Mardi Gras celebration west of the Mississippi River takes place in San Luis Obispo, California. Thousands of people crowd the city's streets to watch a parade of fancy floats and costumed krewe members.

Residents of Galveston, Texas, celebrate Mardi Gras with parades, beauty contests, masked balls, and pancake-flipping contests.

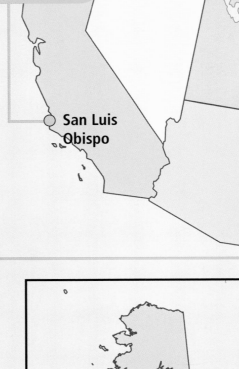

San Luis Obispo

In **rural** areas of Louisiana, Cajun communities celebrate Mardi Gras in a special way. Adults dress up in costumes. They travel together from farm to farm begging for food. At the end of the day, all the food that was collected is used to make a huge shared meal.

The people of St. Louis, Missouri, celebrate Mardi Gras in the historic neighborhood of Soulard. Their outdoor party includes a parade and live music.

In Mobile, Alabama, Mardi Gras is celebrated with grand parades and a special ball. People eat Moon pies during Carnival. Moon pies are small cakes filled with cream and chocolate.

More than twenty Mardi Gras parades are held along the Mississippi Gulf Coast. Cities, such as Biloxi, Gulfport, and Pass Christian, host festive parties.

St. Louis

Rural Louisiana

Mobile

Mississippi Gulf Coast

Galveston

0   250   500 miles

N

Maskers and Throws

People wear masks that hide their faces.

Crazy Costumes and Mysterious Masks

The costumes of Carnival are some of the fanciest in the world. Krewe members who are part of the parades wear colorful costumes that match the themes of their floats. These people are called maskers because they wear masks that hide their faces. People watching the parades also wear costumes. Some costumes include unicorns, clowns, princesses, and cowboys. Some maskers plan their outfits months in advance.

Mardi Gras gives people the opportunity to act and dress differently than they normally act and dress.

Ceramic masks are put on display at Mardi Gras.

Throw Something

Throws are special Mardi Gras **souvenirs**. As floats parade down the streets of New Orleans, maskers toss all kinds of throws to the crowd. The most common throws include beaded necklaces, plastic cups, and **doubloons**. Almost everyone watching a Mardi Gras parade will catch a throw.

People use beads to make Mardi Gras necklaces and bracelets. Each year, a different kind of bead is most popular.

Parade spectators try to catch beads thrown by people on parade floats.

Rhythm and Royalty

Street performers play jazz music and blues songs.

Jazzing it Up

New Orleans is known as the birthplace of jazz music. It is easy to see why. Loud, lively jazz music can be heard all over the city during Carnival and Mardi Gras. Street performers, marching bands, and other musical groups play jazz music and blues songs throughout the days and nights.

New Orleans has a Mardi Gras theme song. This song is called "If Ever I Cease to Love." The words of this song are well known throughout the city.

The music of Mardi Gras was an inspiration to jazz musicians like Louis Armstrong.

If Ever I Cease to Love

If ever I cease to love,
If ever I cease to love,
May oysters have legs,
And cows lay eggs,
If ever I cease to love

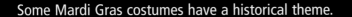

King for a Day

Each Carnival krewe has its own royalty. Each krewe chooses one king and one queen to be part of the krewe's parade. Each year, they appear at the beginning of the parade, before the other floats and bands. The royal couple is also important at the ball. Some krewes have princes, princesses, maids, and other royal court members as well. The king of the Rex krewe is the most important Mardi Gras king.

The leader of every krewe is called the captain. The captain oversees the krewe's activities. The captain chooses the king and queen, and organizes the parade.

Some Mardi Gras costumes have a historical theme.

Colors and Cakes

The colors of Mardi Gras are the colors of royalty.

Royal Colors

The official colors of Mardi Gras are purple, green, and gold. These colors were chosen by the Rex krewe in 1872. That year, the Russian grand duke, Alexis Romanoff, visited New Orleans for Mardi Gras. The Rex krewe wanted to honor the grand duke by using his royal colors. Purple represents justice, green represents **faith**, and gold represents power.

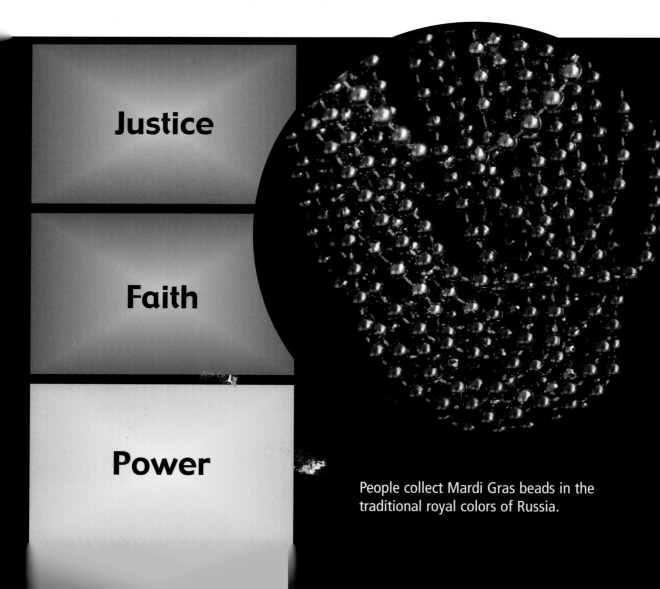

Justice

Faith

Power

People collect Mardi Gras beads in the traditional royal colors of Russia.

King Cakes

King cakes are a favorite treat during Carnival. The cakes are baked into the shape of a crown. Their taste is similar to that of cinnamon buns. King cakes are decorated with purple, green, and gold icing. A tiny, plastic doll is hidden inside each cake. The person who finds the doll must buy the next King cake for the group.

In New Orleans, more than 750,000 King cakes are eaten each year during Carnival.

Bakeries in New Orleans ship King cakes to all parts of the world.

For More Information

Mardi Gras is considered a favorite holiday because it is all about having fun. Many books and Web sites help explain this special time of year. To learn more about Mardi Gras, you can borrow books from a library or search the Internet.

Books

Read these books to find out more about Mardi Gras and New Orleans.

Landau, Elaine. *Mardi Gras: Parades, Costumes, and Parties.* New York: Enslow Publishers, Inc., 2002.

Prentzas, G.S. *New Orleans.* New York: Children's Press, 1999.

Web Sites

Share Mardi Gras with schools in New Orleans.
Mardi Gras on the Net
www.holidays.net/mardigras

Find more information about krewes and throws.
A Guide to Mardi Gras
www.fattuesday.com

Research information on Mardi Gras and New Orleans using an online encyclopedia such as Encarta.
Encarta
www.encarta.com

Imagine if...

Krewes must do a great deal of planning to prepare for Carnival and Mardi Gras. Imagine that you and your friends are forming your own krewe.

- Many krewes are named after the gods of myths and legends. Choose a name for your group.
- Each krewe picks a new theme for Carnival every year. Choose a theme for your group.
- Some krewes invite celebrities to be the kings and queens of their balls. Who will you invite to your ball? Make plans for decorations, music, food, and guests for your ball.
- What play could your krewe perform? Write a play and make plans to perform the play.
- What sort of throws will you toss to the crowds?
- Design a float for your krewe's parade.

What You Have Learned

1 Mardi Gras means "Fat Tuesday" in the French language.

2 Mardi Gras always takes place on the day before Ash Wednesday.

3 Carnival is the season leading up to Mardi Gras.

4 Krewes are special groups that organize balls and parades.

5 French settlers brought the Mardi Gras tradition to the United States in 1699.

6 People on floats toss souvenirs called throws to parade watchers.

More Facts to Know

- Mardi Gras officially ends at midnight.

- Mardi Gras is always the last day before Lent begins. This is 46 days before Easter Sunday.

- Mardi Gras is also called Shrove Tuesday.

- The day before Mardi Gras is called Lundi Gras, which means "Fat Monday" in the French language.

- Carnival celebrations take place all over the world. Some of the largest celebrations are held in Trinidad and Tobago, and in Brazil.

- The way to get more throws at a Mardi Gras parade is to yell, "Throw me something, mister!" This is a traditional Mardi Gras cry.

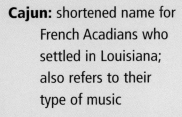

Words to Know

Cajun: shortened name for French Acadians who settled in Louisiana; also refers to their type of music

Christians: people who believe in Jesus Christ and follow his teachings

discrimination: when a certain group of people will not accept other people because of skin color or social class

doubloons: gold coins from Spain

faith: belief in someone or something, such as a leader or a religion

floats: a moving display in a parade

krewes: clubs that organize balls and parades for Carnival

Lent: for Christians, the 40-day period of fasting and praying before Easter

luxuries: nice things that are not really needed

rural: country area

settlers: people who move to live in a new country or area

souvenirs: items that are reminders of a place or event

theme: idea or topic

Index

ML   4/04